My first dictation

Tips from the "Tippse" for future „dictators"

Irmely Fannis

Worpswede / Germany, March 2023

irmely@fannis.com

Bibliographical information of the German national library (Deutsche Nationalbibliothek): The German national library lists this publication in the German national bibliography; detailed bibliographical data available in the internet at http.//dnb.dnb.de.

Maker and publisher: BoD – Books on Demand, Norderstedt / Germany

ISBN: 978-3-7519-6914-7

Irmely Fannis

My first dictation

Tips from the "Tippse" for future "dictators"

Contents

1. Thoughts before the first dictation

1.1 The suitable dictation device

In general, you should not use analogue dictation devices any longer, but only digital ones. That is not only good for the environment, but also good for yourself, for dictations which are transferred on a digital way can be finished much more earlier than dictations on analogue tapes, which first of all you have to send via postal shipping or courier service to your typist. So, analogue dictation devices are not sustainable and still only should be used if your typist is in house with you or sits even next to you – but then you normally don't need a dictation device at all, you can dictate directly into the computer, with or without your typist.

The digital dictation device minimum should have following features:

- you can hold it nicely in your hand,
- it is easy to use,
- it has enough space also for longer dictations,

- it offers the possibility to send the finished dictation directly out from the dictation device to your typist on a safe way.

This safe way is very important, especially if you work together with an external typing office. Already in the beginning you must make sure that you not only can trust the typist him-/herself and his/her signature under your non-disclosure agreement, but also the way you and the typist are communicating and exchanging documents and tapes must be safe in all circumstances.

You should not buy an expensive dictation device with a huge range of additional features that you have to "study" first before you can start at all.

And never ever try to use "speech to text", hoping that by using that you need no typist. These programs are still not sophisticated and cause more work than they are helpful.
The reworking of the text, produced this way, is hard and needs more time than typing the text from the beginning.

Additionally, first of all, you have to "teach" the program your individual vocabulary to avoid that all spoken words are double Dutch to the program.

Recently, I can see more and more often the practice even to publish a text without any reworking, so the text is double Dutch also to the reader and addressee – to whom maybe you want to sell something – so you show towards your potential customer your disrespect and by that make sure that he never will be your customer!

The same problem is also with translation programs without text revision by a human translator (especially Chinese fashion companies are practicing this bad habit).

Also, you should not buy a dictation device that is only one part of a complete dictation program of one single producer, who uses his own internal software, that he developed himself, for all his devices. Then you are bound from the beginning to also buy the transcription device from the same producer due to universal "listening" devices / software are not able to "hear" this brand-dictation. But only very view offices and typists are using this specific brand product, so your choice to find the suitable office / typist is limited from the day one. Furthermore, you are at the mercy of the price policy of this one producer.

Better are dictation devices that produce dictations as general and internationally valid audio files in MP3, RAW etc., which can be transferred to the typist, can be converted there if necessary, or directly can be written.

Meanwhile, you also can dictate directly into your computer or into your smartphone, iPhone, iPad or tablet etc., but for longer dictations that is not very convenient. Here you should still prefer the dictation devices (also very good virtual ones, e.g., from the Australian software house NCH). Good dictation device suppliers also offer the chance to lend or test a dictation device without any costs for a special time before you buy it.

1.2 Thoughts about the text itself

Unfortunately, we all are undergoing an immense time pressure. Therefore, it is important to convey your message concisely.

Avoid unnecessary repetitions and filler words, they only take time, but consider the most important message of your text. This message you repeat and paraphrase a view times. But don't overdo, otherwise your text will land in the next corner of the addressee.

Use a direct, clear, common speech, avoid specific loanwords, if they are not necessary. Use the wording you also use in oral dialogs. If you use too much seldom loanwords, you show your addressee in an indirect way, how smart you are and how stupid he is. And it makes your addressee – who maybe could be your next customer – very angry if he must look up each second word, to understand your message after all.

But of course – if you are, e.g., a physician and address your text to your medical colleague – you speak and write to him in your both medical jargons.

Avoid too long sentences with a lot of embedded sentences. At the end you – and your reader – both of you have forgotten in the end how the sentence was starting. That is confusing. Use short, clear sentences.

Consider if you want to address the addressee normally or more privately.

Only "old stagers" of dictations are able to develop the text during the dictation. Beginners should minimum minute a view keywords, better even prepare a "golden thread", a guideline on which they can "make their hand over hand" during the dictation.

Imagine, the addressee of your text sits directly in front of you – and instead of writing him you just tell him, what you want to tell him. This way the dictation is much easier and faster done.

Consider, how you want to send the text (letter, fax, or email etc.) and how the text should be formatted.

1.3 Choice of the suitable typist / office

If your friend / girlfriend, mama, or colleague already declared him-/herself ready to type your text or if you know already exactly to which office you want to give the order for the task, you can jump this part.

But if you still have to choose, you should consider the following:

Very important is that the communication between you and your typist / your external office is working properly to agree and set obligingly deadlines, prices, formatting, etc.
Therefore, you should always choose an office and typists with the same mother tongue as you speak yourself, to avoid misunderstandings just from the start.

Meanwhile many low-cost suppliers from East Asia are on the market, who offer typing services. Here you must watch out! Their prices are matchless at first glance, but their price policy is inscrutable due to many services that normally are included in the price of a typing office (formatting, wording help, storage, printing, modifications, proofreading etc.) are charged additionally, so you must pay at the end much more than you thought in the beginning, only seeing the low basic prices.

And often the quality of the written text is also not good enough and needs a lot of reworking, what is causing time and money again.

All these things you can and must discuss with an office that communicates in your native language – with an, e.g., Vietnamese office you can eventually discuss that only in English, a language that is not the mother tongue of both of you. So, misunderstandings are inevitable, maybe, it is even not possible at all to communicate with the other side.

You should choose an office that is in the market already successfully for long time, thus long-term experience and excellent quality is guaranteed.

You should choose an office that invoices after performance done (e.g., tape minutes or typed chars) and not after performance time. It should be an all-inclusive price, including formatting and wording help, proofreading and correction, reworkings, printouts, storage, etc. .

Best for you is an office that worked already often in the field in which you are busy too.

2. The dictation

2.1. In general

Do not be afraid to speak into your dictation device, but remember the "golden threat" that you have prepared, then I am confident that you will do it well.

By experience I know that many highly remunerated and esteemed managers are dyslexics after all, whose asses are covered by their typists who iron their defects out in silence. And what they do for them, they will do for you too – and you even are no dyslexic, so you have no reason to be scared at all.

And – we live in the era of IT and computers and not any longer in the era of the Adler-typewriters by which you had to rub each fault laboriously out from the blueprint and the original (first) paper. Later on you could correct the original by Tipp-Ex. To say it more exactly: Tipp-Ex was a "revolution" in the typists' offices, and Adler-typewriters were already long time "out" at that time. Then the first electric typewriters were in the offices, another "revolution", before then the first computers (first as automatic typewriter with a huge screen) found their way into the offices.

At the time of Adler-typewriters and later Tipp-Ex only small corrections could be made. Today it is no problem to exchange even whole passages in a text, and it is common to exchange passages as often as you want it.

So, you see, nowadays everything is technically possible and is not causing any extra-time and extra-work to produce exactly that kind of text you want.

2.2. All things dictations

When I was writing this book I was overthinking if it is necessary and not too silly to write the following, but my experiences with people who practice these described behaviors tell me that I should minimum mention these problems marginally.

I know that you are a nice and polite person and will never ever do any of these things I describe now. So don't mind if I say "you" in the following text, I don't address you personally.

Normally it should be clear - and needless to say -, that already the respectful interaction between you and your typist demands that you don't cough loudly or blow your nose suddenly into the microphone during the dictation without any prior warning, and that you don't eat during the dictation and speak with a full mouth.

Also you must watch out that you end a sentence in a way that it is matching the beginning of the sentence. Otherwise, that is nerving your typist a lot, if he/she must overthink with each sentence to better take the beginning or the end of the sentence to continue and correct it in a proper way. He/she cannot write the text fluidly, but always after a few words must stop the tape and must solve this problem before he/she can continue. That is especially a problem with very long sentences.

You also show no respect if you transfer the dictation to your typist just short before the deadline you both had agreed before.

Example:
One week before, you agree with your typist the deadline when the finished text shall be in your lawyer's office, e.g., Monday morning next week. You say that it's very important to keep this deadline due to your lawyer must keep a deadline given him from court. You say that the volume of the dictation will be approximately 30 minutes.
Until Friday evening your typist got nothing from you, only your short information that you will start with the dictation now and will have finished it maybe Saturday noon.

Thus, you take it for granted that your typist will work during the weekend and therefore cannot make any other plans for the weekend. You were not asking your typist before if that is possible for him/her for that weekend.

Saturday noon you send the message to your typist that you did not start yet, but that you will start in one hour. Saturday evening you send the first five minutes of the dictation with the message that the rest will follow tomorrow. Sunday noon your typist still didn't receive the rest. At 10 p.m. on Sunday evening, you send the finished dictation to your typist. The rest volume is not – as agreed before – 25 minutes, but 50 minutes, the double volume. Your instruction to the typist is to send the finished text directly to your lawyer, without any proofreading from your side before, for you want to go to sleep now.

Thus, you take it for granted that your typist will work during the whole night to make sure that the text will be in your lawyer's office on Monday morning.

If that is happening one time your typist will turn a blind eye to it – due to it can happen to each of us, that something comes between that prevents us from keeping a deadline -, but if that is happening always and becomes almost routine, it is simply rank and inappropriate. You can be happy if your typist is not quitting the co-operation, but only asks you for a date to have a serious discussion.

Regarding 50 minutes dictation time – that sounds not to be so much. But 50 minutes dictation time are, incl. formatting, minimum 200 minutes typing time (three hours, 20 minutes) if the dictation is fluid and well understandable. But if the dictation is slipshod, hardly understandable and dictated without keeping any dictation rules these 50 minutes dictation need already a typing time of 500 minutes, (eight hours, 20 minutes) due to it is necessary to rewind the tape again and again, to have endless researching and queries, before the typist can finish the text.

These typing times you always must keep in mind when you agree a deadline with your typist.

The quality of the dictation is also important when your typist is calculating the price that you have to pay. For a well understandable dictation from an experienced "routine-dictator" (e.g., lawyer) that is finished without any revision needs I charge, e.g., 1.50 – 2.00 Euro for each tape minute. For a troublesome, very bad dictation that needs a lot of modifications, research, reworking again and again, consultations etc., - so it needs a complete editing after all -, I charge 1 Cent for each typed character (incl. space chars) of the final document. Fast that then can be ten times more than the sum the routineer must pay.

Within this margin there are a lot of variations.

For you important is to know that an experienced, professional typist is taking it for granted to catch you if you fall, as he/she is doing it with each dictator, who even can be a dyslexic. Your text will always be perfect, no matter how good or bad your dictation was.
And of course, that all is a question of the price, that you are willing to pay, and the respectful, faithful co-operation between you and your typist.

Also that is a reason, not to choose the first available and cheapest typing office, but the more experienced one that is already long time on the market for it delivers superb quality at a reasonable price.

And of course, that is also a question of trust which is very important especially in this field. For this one you have sympathy, but not for the other one. With this one you can imagine a trustful co-operation, but in no case with the other one.

To a typist with a relationship of personal trust you can commit your weak points, so he/she can bear that in mind all over again, if you ask her/him for assistance.

And, also important is to make sure that you will not be disturbed during your dictation.

So, you see – in principle nothing can go wrong. If you keep that in mind you can start with your work at ease.

2.3. Dictation rules

2.3.1 Speak distinctly

Speak distinctly in your normal speech tempo, not too loud, not too low. Many people start to mumble during the dictation if something, what they just dictate, is painful for them to speak out, or if they are not sure, if that, what they just are dictating, is correct so or not. Fish or cut bait, either you say something, or you don't say it. To mumble under the motto "I'm not sure if I should say that" is not getting you anywhere. That is a point that you should well overthink when you prepare your "golden thread", but not during your dictation.

2.3.2 Proper winding and rewinding of the tape

The exact winding forward and back you will learn over time. Soon you will be able to do that in your sleep. But in the beginning it is hard to rewind exactly to that point from where you want to continue the already dictated text with other words, overwriting the former text. The same hard it is in the beginning to jump forward exactly to that point where you had stopped the tape. The more you change the text you had already spoken on the tape, the harder it is to find the exact points to continue.

Here it helps to listen at the end, when you have accomplished your dictation, once more to the whole tape from the beginning to hear if everything is exactly at the place you wanted it to be.

If that is not working well even after your third try, it is better you hand this task over to your typist, by saying during the dictation:

"Stop. At that point where I said ..., please insert ... instead, and after that continue at the end with .... Continue."

One of my clients for over ten years up to now is not able to wind forward and rewind exactly, but is also too proud to follow my tip, for the th nks that that tip is not necessary for him. He always rewinds much too far back, with the result that thus many words and even whole sentences are lost, what causes many unnecessary queries from my side.

2.3.3 Instructions during the dictation

Instructions, regarding the whole dictation, please direct at the very beginning, e.g., which formatting (full justification or running text) or character font / character seize and what line spacing you want.

This is not essential, most of the "dictators" delegate these decisions fully to the typist of their trust, he/she knows the best what looks nice, or which legal or regulatory requirements must be kept.

At the very start of your dictation, you must tell your typist also, who shall be the addressee of your text and how you want to transfer the text (postal letter, fax, email).

Normally you must not dictate punctuation marks, that is doing the typist by him-/herself. But if something shall be highlighted or if the following text shall be formatted in the form of a table or list etc., you must give the applicable instruction. If you give this instruction during the dictation, say "Stop", give the instruction, and then say "Continue".

Always say "Stop" and "Continue" if you want to tell your typist something. Without this "Stop" and "Continue" your typist always thinks that that what you just said is part of the text he/she is preparing. When he/she is checking that the last words are not part of the dictation, he/she has typed already for a while and has wasted time unnecessar ly.

One time that happened to me already. I was typing and typing, until I checked that the last words were not matching the text before and had to realize that my customer meanwhile was talking on the phone to somebody and was not dictating any more, without saying "Stop" before.

Also important is that you say "End of the dictation" when a dictation is finished especially if there are more than one dictation on the tape.

2.3.4 Proper spelling

Not only with the addressee, also later in the text it is very important that you spell names, addresses etc. in a proper way. Do not say just "a", "b" etc., but always prolong the character into a complete word, so in our example you could say "Alpha", "Bee Gees" etc. or something else what just comes into your mind when you hear that character.

The reason for that kind of spelling is that some chars sound nearly the same, e.g., "b" and "d" or even in some cases "e". That is no problem with a word that is known, but with an unknown word that is a big problem for the typist, who must research or ask you unnecessarily before he/she can continue with typing. Thanks to the internet, nowadays it is more comfortable to research names and addresses. But that is only working if you research a generally known name (e.g., a company name, a public character, etc.). But if you want to write a letter to your granny your typist cannot know the correct spelling of the name and address and needs to ask you unnecessarily.

This kind of spelling you should use generally, not only during dictations, but also each time when it is important for you that your conversation partner is understanding a word properly, e.g., on the phone.

When it comes to spell a word, you always should use this kind of spelling method.

As time goes by, you will be able to do that blindfolded. But until then you always should have a small cheat sheet in your pocket on which you have noted, e.g., the following, what is the internationally known and used spelling method:

A	Alpha	N	November
B	Bravo	O	Oscar
C	Charlie	P	Papa
D	Delta	Q	Quebec
E	Echo	R	Romeo
F	Foxtrott	S	Sierra
G	Golf	T	Tango
H	Hotel	U	Uniform
I	India	V	Victor
J	Juliet	W	Whiskey
K	Kilo	X	X-ray
L	Lima	Y	Yankee
M	Mike	Z	Zulu

That is just an example. You can, of course, use your own words if you want.

3. After dictation

The experienced "multi-dictator" (e.g., lawyer, expert, architect, surveyor, etc.) has completed his work when he/she has accomplished the dictation. They themselves only maybe still add or correct smaller things in the transferred Word® file. They had been so well prepared and are so experienced that their text is just "standing" from the beginning. That is the reason why external offices and internal typists like to work for this clientele: Their orders are fast done, without any research and questionings. The interpersonal dealing is respectful and sympathetic.

But there are also the persons who hold back, who just have sketchy ideas and need a "scaffold" for their ideas. They are not well prepared, but first want to see, what they have dictated already and what still is missing. They want to see if the structure of the text is good this way or if they must / want to change the complete structure. During their proofreading they haven thousands of new ideas, what they still want to insert into the text and what they absolutely want to reject, they have thousand new ideas for an alternative wording and sequence. In extreme cases, in the end there is no analogy any more between the final version and the initial, original version. The whole procedure can last months and months.

Here it is necessary that your typist is patient and sympathetic and assists you if you ask him/her for help.

As a dictation newbie you cannot dictate like a professional of course. But that is no problem. As you see, there are many kinds of dictation. Just start and say "what comes into your head" – as I wrote already, everything is possible.

3.1 Effective proofreading

From experience I know that the following procedure is the fastest and most result-producing one when it comes to proofreading:

Your typist transfers your finished dictation as PDF-file to you.

I send the dictations as PDF-file, firstly due to not all customers have access to Word®-programs to read the text, and secondly due to many customers just are not able to stop their bad behavior to put corrections or modifications themselves into the Word®-document. Then they dictate modifications and corrections, that I shall write, but take as base the document, that they themselves have changed already. By doing so they assume of course that I must take a look at their modifications if everything is correct how they were doing t themselves – sometimes their modifications are just only a proposal, and I shall decide how to say it the best. So I now must read the whole text again, have to compare each sentence in the different versions of the document, have, eventually, to modify their corrections and have not only to do the corrections and modifications that he/she has dictated just, but also have to take care, that the whole sentence is now in the final version, what is a mixture between the first, initial text, the modifications and corrections of the customer himself in the document and the modifications and corrections what he/she dictated at last. Especially with long texts this is very laborious and needs a lot of checking back to convert all versions of the document into one final version, for additionally most of the customers also cannot handle the program in the revision mode.

So please, my dear "dictators", either I do the corrections after your dictation, or you yourself are correcting and modifying your text – but not we both together in the same text at the same time!

Therefore, I'm sending the document as PDF-file, thus something like that cannot happen at all.

And – as I said already – it is not useful at all to use the revision mode of the Word®-program if you are not very experienced in that. And if you are not using it, your typist should not use it too. Only if you are a professional and well experienced Word®-user, that makes any sense and you and your typist can accomplish your revision works in a fast and effective way. For all other "dictators" it is still better just to mark the regarding passages in, e.g., yellow.

So, after you now got the PDF-file with the written dictation, you mark and number your single modification points all the way through in the PDF-document and dictate to each number your modification or correction. Then you send this PDF-document with the numbers of the revision points and the tape with dictated revision points to me.

I rework the initial, original version of the text accordingly and send you the modified text back, again as PDF-file, version 2, but I am keeping the initial, first version, if you later still need passages of this version.

If you want, you can still modify your text again the same way. This procedure you and your typist can practice a view times, until the final version is "standing", and you are fully satisfied.

4. Conclusion

This stupid slogan "No one is born a master" I keep to myself at this place. In my whole life I experienced again and again that trial and error is the faster and more effective method, faster than any studying before doing.

So, just do it - your typist is at hand to catch you if you fall.

If you still are skeptical and gaze at your dictation device you are like my granny, who once was gazing at the phone, into which she was shouting due to her conversation partner was so far away. The trolley she was calling "die Elektrische" (electric tram) in opposition to the cable car, pulled by horses – how she knew it from her childhood. For my granny a tv or a fridge had been mysterious and funny things, she was a little afraid of long time.

Today, the technology is developing in a speed that makes us feel dizzy sometimes, and each day it makes us again to start as beginners with just new devices. Be confident, for we all are beginners.

So, if your heart was sinking in a big black hole as once the heart of my granny, I advise you to stop the whole plan for a while and let the project sink in – if your time schedule is tolerating that -, to start afterwards with fresh confidence again. I know that you can do it and will master it – in principle that is really very easy.

Along these lines – all the best and Godspeed!

Your

"Tippse"